Box Turtles

A Box Turtle Owner's Guide

Box Turtle care, where to buy, types, behavior, cost, handling, husbandry, diet, and much more included!

By Lolly Brown

Foreword

Turtles are fast becoming a popular pet choice all over the world, and Box Turtles are among the best choices for a beginner's pet turtle in the United States.

Native to the United States and Mexico, Box Turtles have long been bred and raised by keepers in captivity, which means that they are easy to come by if you are looking for a pet turtle. They are also a fairly gentle and hardy breed as compared to many other species, making them one of the more popular choices for turtle pets in the United States.

There are different kinds of Box Turtles, and these are distinguished by type and their region of origin. And while many turtles will never be fully accommodating to being handled by or socializing with humans, Box Turtles bred in captivity and that have grown familiar to the presence of humans are at least moderately sociable, and are tolerant of human presence.

Easygoing, docile, quiet, non-aggressive, are just some of the words one can use to describe a Box Turtle. If you have ever considered keeping a Box Turtle for a pet, then this book is for you.

Table of Contents

Introduction

Reptiles are fast growing in popularity as pets – people view them as more quiet and easily maintained pets as compared to the more traditional human companions like cats and dogs. And easily topping that list of popular reptile pets are turtles, including the gentle, fairly hardy, and comparably easy to care for Box Turtles.

Before you go out and get a Box Turtle for your pet, however, it is important to sit down and do your research, and assess objectively whether or not this really is the best pet for you. Box Turtles are complex creatures and they require a very specialized kind of care that can be quite expensive. Don't be fooled by those who try to sell you on

Box Turtles by saying that they are low maintenance pets. It's true that you can pretty much leave these turtles to their own devices as long as you give them a good enclosure and feed them a proper diet, but turtle enclosures need regular cleaning and a specific environment in terms of temperature, humidity, and bedding or substrate; and some turtles are notoriously finicky eaters. You will also probably need to bring them to a veterinarian every so often – and all of these can easily total a good amount each year. And with Box Turtles living for as long as 45 years on the average, this easily translates to years of daily care and maintenance costs.

Box Turtles are certainly amazing creatures, beautiful and full of stolid character, which is why they deserve careful consideration before you bring one of these unique creatures home. This is not a pet to bring home on a whim.

Glossary of Box Turtle Terms

Anterior – Towards the front or head

Basking – Behavior designed to gain maximum absorption of heat from the sun

Beak – The hard outer covering of the jaws

Bridges – Sides of a shell that connects the carapace and plastron

Carapace – The hard, body upper shell of a turtle

Chelonian – A shield reptile, including turtles, tortoises and terrapins

Clutch – Collective term for eggs

Costal – Series of plates between the side and middle of the shell

Diurnal – Active during the day

Dorsal – Upper part

Ecosystem – Natural coexistence between organisms and the environment

Ectoparasite – Parasites that live on the outside of a host's body

Ectotherm – Organisms that rely upon environmental sources for the regulation of its body temperature

Endangered species – Species that are found in such small numbers that they are at risk of extinction

Endemic – Species restricted to a specific geography

Endoparasite – Internal parasite

Endotherm – Organisms which self-generates heat by metabolism, e.g., mammals

Filter – Device used to extract impurities from air or water

Gestation – The period between egg fertilization and egg laying

Gravid - Pregnant

Habitat – The external environment in which an organism lives

Hatchling – Young turtle after it leaves the egg, or any juvenile tortoise until 6 months

Herpetology – Study of reptiles and amphibians

Hibernation – Winter dormancy

Hinge – Mobile suture which enables the shell to be closed

Incubation – Developmental phase of an egg or embryo prior to hatching, requiring specific temperatures

Juvenile – Not sexually mature

Mesic – Intermediate humidity habitat

Microclimate – The climate that immediately surrounds an organism

Nocturnal – Active at night

Omnivore – Feeds on both plants and animals

Oviparous – Egg-laying

Plastron – The bottom surface of a chelonian shell

Salmonella – Disease commonly carried by turtles

Scute – Horny plates of a chelonian shell

Semi-terrestrial – An animal that lives on land but also goes into the water

Substrate – Flooring material for a Turtle's habitat, cage or enclosure

Temperate – Regions with well-defined seasonal changes, and where summer and winter seasons occur

Terrestrial – Not aquatic, living on land

Vivarium – Indoor artificial environment that houses animals

Chapter One: Understanding Box Turtles

Box Turtles, also sometimes known as Shelled Box Turtles or Crescent Turtles, of the genus Terrapene, are a species native to the United States and Mexico. There are four species of Box Turtles spread out over different regions, including the Common Box Turtle, the Coahuilan Box Turtle, the Spotted Box Turtle, and the Ornate Box Turtle.

Box Turtles have a distinctive dome-shaped shell with a hinged bottom that allows the turtle to retract into its shell and close it tightly against predators. They can literally "box themselves in" – thus accounting for their name.

Box Turtles have easily become very popular pets in recent years – they are fairly hardy, and compared to most other turtles and tortoises, their habitat and dietary needs are pretty straightforward, though no less complex and specific. But they are quiet creatures, and fairly small, so many people have opted to keep them as pets when dogs or cats simply won't do.

It is important to remember, however, that Box Turtles are not like traditional pets in that they will never demonstrate affection to you as their keeper. In fact, they don't even appreciate being handled too often and too much, and would far prefer being left alone. These are solitary creatures, and although they are gentle and mild-mannered, they can also be easily stressed by too much socialization and major changes in their habitat. Box Turtles like their privacy. If you are the type who likes demonstrative affection between you and your pet, then a Box Turtle is probably not the best choice for you. For that matter, if you are the type who shuns the kind of long, term daily responsibility of maintenance and upkeep that this quiet little turtle needs, then you're better off looking for another pet.

So when does a Box Turtle make a good pet? There is really no easy and fast answer – Box Turtles make great pets for those who want Box Turtles as pets. But a caveat to this is that the person must fully understand what it means to care for one of these amazing creatures. With a fully informed choice, Box Turtles can make amazing lifelong pets and companions.

Summary of Box Turtle Facts

Basic Box Turtle Information

Kingdom: Animalia

Phylum: Chordata

Class: Reptilia

Order: Testudines

Suborder: Cryptodira

Family: Emydidae

Genus: Terrapene

Species: Terrapene Carolina, Terrapene Coahuila, Terrapene Nelsoni, Terrapene Ornata

Regions of Origin:

- Common Box Turtles – South-Central, Eastern, and South Eastern parts of the United States, the Yucatan Peninsula and North Eastern parts of Mexico
- Ornate Box Turtle – South central and Southwestern parts of the United States, including adjacent parts of Mexico
- Spotted Box Turtle – North-Western Mexico

- Coahuilan Box Turtle – Cuatro Cienegas Basin in Coahuila, Mexico

Primary Habitat: Box Turtles occupy a wide variety of habitats depending on the type and region of origin, and can include grasslands, Mesic woodlands, semi-desert with occasional rainfall, or marshes

Description: Characterized by a domed shell with a hinged bottom. They don't have teeth, but have a rigid beak with upper and lower jaws covered by sharp, horny ridges which they use to eat tough and fibrous vegetation. Shell color patterns differ depending on the species, and helps them blend better into their environment. While the turtle's vertebra is rigid and elongated in the central part of the shell, it is small and flexible in the neck and tail, for easier movement.

Male irises are red or orange, and a female's is brown or yellow. But a better way to distinguish them by gender is the plastron, or the bottom shell. This is more concave in males for easier mating. Box Turtles have a hinged joint at the bottom which they can close tightly after hiding within its shell to serve as protection against predators.

Length: In general, adults range from 4-7 inches across the carapace, but there are still variations in size among the different species.

Weight: 1-2 lbs

Conservation Status:

- Common Box Turtles – Vulnerable
- Ornate Box Turtle – Near threatened
- Spotted Box Turtle – No official status due to lack of study
- Coahuilan Box Turtle – Endangered

Health Conditions: Swollen and closed eyes, Ear abscesses, Parasites, Shell and Skin Problems, Respiratory Infection, Metabolic Bone Disease

Lifespan: average 40-50 years

Origin and Distribution

Box turtles are a genus native to the United States and Mexico. There are four recognized species of box turtles: the Common box turtle, the Coahuilan box turtle, the Spotted box turtle,, and the Ornate box turtle.

The most widely distributed species is the common box turtle, which is found in South-Central, Eastern, and the South Eastern parts of the United States, as well as in the Yucatan peninsula and the North Eastern parts of Mexico.

The Ornate Box turtle is endemic to the South-central and South Western parts of the United States and adjacent parts of Mexico. The Spotted box turtle is endemic only to

North-Western Mexico, while the Coahuilan box turtle is only found in the Cuatro Cienegas Basin in Coahuila, Mexico.

Box turtles occupy a wide variety of habitats – which varies depending on the species and the season, so there is not really an identifiable standard habitat for the box turtle. In general, however, box turtles can be found in Mesic or a moderately moist habitat, or an ecology with a well=balanced supply of moisture. Some species, however, can also be found in grasslands or even in semi-desert areas. Interestingly, the box turtle is the official reptile of at least four U.S. states: North Carolina, Tennessee, Missouri, and Kansas.

Species and Subspecies of Box Turtles

Below we take a look at the species and subspecies of the box turtle, including their current state of distribution.

1. Common Box Turtle – Its official status is "vulnerable." While the common box turtle was once pretty widespread and common, their numbers have dwindled drastically due to various causes such as the loss of habitat, getting run over by cars, and illegal collection for the pet trade. There are six recognized subspecies of the

Common Box Turtle, most of which are named for regions in which they are endemic to, including:

a. Eastern Box Turtle – Mainly located in the eastern United States, the eastern box turtle is one of the more well-known subspecies. Officially, its status is "vulnerable."

b. Florida Box Turtle – The Florida Box Turtle is located almost exclusively in its namesake state of Florida, though sometimes it can also be found in southern Georgia. Officially, its status is "least concern."

c. Gulf Coast Box Turtle – Found mainly along the Gulf of Mexico, and in the areas between the states of Louisiana and Florida.

d. Three Toed Box Turtle – The three-toed box turtle has been found to be more tolerant of new surroundings, and are therefore regarded as the better subspecies to keep as pets. It has been recently suggested, however, that this subspecies characterized by the iconic three-toed hind legs might actually be a separate species altogether.

e. Mexican Box Turtle – Endemic to Mexico, the Mexican Box Turtle are rarely seen in the pet trade. Laws are in place to protect this subspecies, by preventing their exportation.

f. Yucatan Box Turtle – This subspecies is endemic to the Yucatan state of Mexico. It does not have an official endangered rating, but their numbers seem to be dwindling, based on local sightings.

2. Spotted Box Turtle – Named for the tiny spots all over its shell, the Spotted Box Turtle has not been well studied as a species. It has no official status due to this lack of study, though there are two recognized subspecies:

    a. Northern Spotted Box Turtle

    b. Southern Spotted Box Turtle

3. Ornate Box Turtle – The Ornate Box Turtle is also sometimes known as the Western Box Turtle. This species is characterized by a flatter appearance in the dome of its shell. There are two recognized subspecies of the Ornate or Western Box Turtle:

    a. Desert Box Turtle – As its name implies, the Desert Box Turtle is located mainly in dryer areas such as Texas, Arizona, and New Mexico.

    b. Ornate Box Turtle – The official status of the Ornate Box Turtle is "near threatened."

4. Coahuilan Box Turtle – Also known as the Aquatic Box Turtle, the Coahuilan Box Turtle is endemic to

Coahuila, Mexico. This is the only known Aquatic box turtle in North America. Its official status is "endangered."

The Asian Box Turtles, on the other hand, of the genus Cuora (North American Box Turtles are of the genus Terrapene) is not as widely available in the pet trade. While similar to the Terrapene or North American box turtle genus in terms of having a hinged and domed shell, the Cuora or Asian Box Turtles also differ in traits and characteristics, from appearance and habitat to personality and diet. There are about twelve species of the Asian box turtle, originating in countries such as China, Indonesia, and the Philippines. Due to the wide diversity of information, however, this genus of box turtle is not covered in this book.

Chapter Two: Things to Know Before Getting a Box Turtle

As with most pets, it is highly recommended that you do your research before you bring home a Box Turtle. As amazing and as beautiful as these creatures are, they do not always make the best pets for everybody. They require very particular care and attention, and their upkeep can be costly. You will need to invest a whole lot of time and energy to making sure that they remain happy and healthy in your care.

Reptiles are often fascinating to children, but right here, it must be emphasized that Box Turtles are not the best pets for children. They require maturity and steady responsibility, and constant handling by children will not make ideal environments for these turtles. And of course, children and other persons with weak immune systems can be susceptible to various diseases that reptiles like Box Turtles can carry, such as Salmonella – particularly if one does not practice proper hygiene, are unable to maintain regular cleaning and maintenance of turtle enclosures, and proper waste disposal.

And children might not be able to appreciate the fact that reptiles like Box Turtles aren't particularly affectionate as pets. They can be quite gentle creatures, but they will not like constant handling and too much stress. If scared or stressed, they could lash out by biting or scratching with their long nails. If you do have a child at home, it is best to ask yourself whether it is a good idea to keep a Box Turtle as a pet in the same environment as your child, and whether it is really the best situation for both turtle and child. If not, then perhaps you would be better off with a less exotic pet such as a dog or cat.

If you do decide on bringing home a Box Turtle as a pet, there are various other considerations to look into before actually bringing one home. Turtles need particular care in terms of diet and habitat. You might also wish to look in your area for veterinarians who have experience dealing with reptiles and Box Turtles in particular, since you would probably be requiring professional medical care at one point

or another. And, of course, turtles are notoriously long-lived
– they might even outlive you! Obviously, this isn't a pet
that you can bring home one day and grow bored of after a
few months or years. They will literally require years,
maybe even decades, of care, housing, and feeding, among
others things.

Some of the other practical considerations for keeping
a Box Turtle are covered in this chapter, including licensing
requirements, projected costs, and the pros and cons of
keeping pet turtles. Read them over and ask yourself again
whether you can objectively say that a Box Turtle would
make the perfect pet for you and your home. And then read
more books and do more research before you finally make
up your mind.

Do You Need a License?

Not all turtles are legal to keep everywhere – and in
fact, it is not legal in the United States to buy or sell pet
turtles whose carapace or upper shells are less than four
inches. This came about because of widespread Salmonella
cases among children in the 60s and 70s, primarily because
of how they handled the turtles, which in most cases
included kissing them.

So be warned that it is illegal to buy a hatchling for a pet if their carapace is less than four inches – whether you are buying from a pet shop or breeder. As for the legality of acquiring and keeping Box Turtles larger than four inches at the carapace – you will still have to check your local laws.

Each state has its own laws regarding keeping wildlife as pets, and it behooves you to look this up *before* you actually purchase your Box Turtle and bring one home. Check with your local legislature regarding what laws apply to your area or region, and pay particular attention to the following:

- If Box Turtles are not endemic to your area, check out the legality of bringing in non-endemic or non-native species into your area or region to keep as pets. This aims to prevent the possibility of foreign species getting into the local ecology and upsetting the natural balance of the prevailing species in your area.
- Even if the sale of an animal is lawful at the point of origin, it might not be legal to transport them across state lines and into your area. Or you may need a permit for such transport. This also applies when importing, exporting, and transporting wildlife across international borders – where a CITES (Convention on International Trade of Endangered Species of Wild Fauna and Flora) permit might be required for specific listed species.

- Conversely, even if it is legal to keep wildlife in your - area provided you have met local requirements like permits and licenses, be careful where you acquire or purchase your Turtle because they might not be legal where they come from. In general, laws prohibit the sale and purchase of Box Turtles or other animals caught in the wild, and only permit the sale and purchase of captive bred animals.

- Check out local laws regarding sale, barter or exchange of animals. The laws in your area might allow keeping Box Turtles as pets, but might prohibit giving them away, breeding them, selling them, or exchanging pets with others. Releasing pets such as Turtles and other reptiles into the wild is also considered by many states as illegal. There could also be a limit on the number of pets allowed per owner.

- Be aware that restrictions might be provided regarding the keeping as pets of animals that have been classified as endangered or threatened. Even if Box Turtles have not been mentioned by name, if their formal classification changes to threatened or endangered – particularly specific types of Box Turtles, then they will certainly fall under this classification and could thereby be considered a protected species. You will probably need to update yourself regularly regarding endangered species listings since this changes overtime, depending on the prevailing numbers of a certain species in the wild.

- Don't forget to check your municipal bylaws, or city and state laws regarding regulations governing the keeping of Box Turtles and other reptiles as pets. Even if your state allows the keeping of Box Turtles as pets, city or municipal laws might prohibit it or consider it illegal, or might prescribe specific requirements such as licenses and permits, fees, etc.

And lastly, please don't forget that all these restrictions – particularly those regarding the transport of reptiles across state lines – applies if you as the owner of a pet turtle are moving your residence to a different location. You will be required to get a permit for transport, and you will surely need to check the prevailing laws in the place you intend to move to, to see whether it would be legal for you to keep your turtle as a pet in your new home. Considering that Box Turtles live for a very long time, this is yet another consideration to factor in before deciding to bring one home as a pet. Remember that there could also be restrictions on giving them away, selling them, or releasing them into the wild. Consider all these carefully to make sure you are ready and willing to take on the considerable, and likely lifelong, responsibility for keeping Box Turtles as pets.

How Many Box Turtles Should You Keep?

If this is your first time to keep Box Turtles as pets –
or any other species of reptiles or turtles as pets, for that
matter – it will probably be best if you stick to one pet at a
time. And no, your Box Turtle will probably not feel all that
lonely for the lack of company. Turtles and Tortoises are, in
the main, solitary creatures, and they will not crave for the
attention and affection of another turtle, or even of you as
their owner, for that matter. Many turtles – particularly
adult males – kept in the same enclosure might even get
aggressive against one another. Or different turtles –
especially different turtle and tortoise species kept together
in one enclosure, could harbor different bacteria that could
make the others sick. So while you could certainly look into
the possibility of keeping more than one turtle – just make
sure that you have sufficient room for them both. Once you
figure out how much work actually goes into the care of just
one turtle, you'll probably agree that one turtle alone is
plenty.

More experienced keepers and hobbyists who
specialize in Box Turtles and other similar reptiles can
certainly keep more than one pet – but this requires years of
experience and knowledge, and a lot of investment in
equipment, space, tools, and practical know-how. If you are
only starting out with your first turtle, give yourself a break
and start by just learning how to care for one Box Turtle.

Another thing you should factor into your decision of keeping more than one Box Turtle is the fact that some states prohibit the captive breeding of turtles, or at least require a license or permit for the captive breeding of reptiles. If you keep a male and female together in one enclosure (one enclosure for each turtle can take up a lot of space – at 10 gallons per inch of carapace), then you have to anticipate that the natural breeding process will take place. Having tiny hatchlings just showing up one day may seem exciting and endearing, but raising those hatchlings take up a lot more work, too – and a lot more space, tools and equipment. And it isn't really that easy to re-home turtles, no matter how amazing creatures they are. Many states also require different permits if you wish to engage in commercial trade in reptiles – which would certainly cover selling captive-bred turtles.

It is always a good idea, when considering the different factors of keeping a Box Turtle as a Pet – to think long term. Forty-five years down the line, is this something that you would still consider appealing? That is how long Box Turtles can live. If you're having second thoughts at this point – think again, and think thrice more. Caring for a turtle means considering their best interests – which in certain cases might mean not keeping them as your personal pet.

Do Box Turtles Get Along with Other Pets?

It is probably best to keep your Box Turtle isolated from other pets. Not only will this keep down chances of bacteria spreading (Box Turtles can sometimes carry bacteria that do not affect them, but which can be lethal to humans, such as Salmonella), but doing so will also ensure their safety, health and wellbeing. Cats, and even dogs, could see your Box Turtle as prey – which means that you'll have to ensure your turtle's safety, particularly when left unsupervised. Coming home to find that your dog or cat has eaten your Box Turtle is a very real possibility unless you have made sure that your turtle's enclosure is safeguarded. To make matters worse, it might also be lethal or poisonous for your dog or cat to ingest a turtle – considering the toxins or other substances that could be fatal to mammals.

The same is also true if you are keeping your Box Turtle in an outdoor enclosure. There are many other wild animals that can see your pet as prey – including wild cats, raccoons, and even Fire Ants. Whatever enclosure you provide them, whether an indoor tank or an outdoor enclosure – their safety should be a paramount concern.

How Much Does it Cost to Keep a Box Turtle?

The cost or purchase price of a Box Turtle can vary depending on whether or not they are native or non-endemic to your region. This would certainly depend on which type of Box Turtle you are looking to purchase, as the different types are usually classified by their region of origin. Generally, though, Box Turtles that are widely available as pets can range in purchase price from $10-50.

They can be bought from pet stores, breeders, or rescues, with the higher price ranges being charged by legitimate breeders. The adoption fee for rescued turtles are often within the same price range as those that you can buy from pet stores, though sometimes rescue turtles can also be offered for adoption by certain shelters for adoption free of charge. Turtles that wind up in rescues are usually former pets of owners who can no longer provide their pets with the care and commitment that they require. In any case, always make sure that you are not purchasing a hatchling or a turtle that is less than 4 inches in carapace length – something that is considered illegal in the United States since 1975.

The price of $10-15 may not seem like much – and certainly far cheaper than the purchase price for many popular cat and dog pet breeds. Much of the cost of keeping a turtle is in the equipment you would need to house them, as well as the yearly recurring costs of upkeep and maintenance. The first year will certainly be more expensive as this is when you will be making investments in good equipment such as an enclosure or habitat. After the first year, costs will begin to level off. In general, the cost of turtle upkeep is not that expensive – they require more in terms of time and commitment than in actual expenses.

A general breakdown of your first year's costs can look something like this:

Initial Costs for a Box Turtle	
Purchase Price	$30-75
Terrarium/Aquarium	$100-200
UV-A and UV-B light source	$20-90
Water dish	$10
Additional terrarium supplies (timers, water heaters, surge protectors, etc.)	$100-200
Initial Veterinarian Checkup	$120
Initial Set Up Cost	$380-695

This does not include the yearly recurring costs that can include the following:

Yearly Recurring Costs for a Box Turtle	
Turtle diet including animal protein, vegetables and turtle feed	$240-480 (at $20-40 per month)
Annual veterinary visits	$20-80
Total Yearly Recurring Costs	$260-560

It's probably best to save up a few hundred dollars before actually purchasing your turtle so that you can immediately set up their new habitat. There are also a lot of great deals in terms of buying turtle food, pellets, and vitamins, and there are certainly ways of keeping down costs so that the monthly expenses are more than reasonable at an average of about $50 a month. It is probably a good idea, though, to keep an emergency fund for unforeseen medical or emergency expenses that have you running to the vet at unexpected moments. Typically, treatments requiring lab tests could run into $100-200 each time. So aside from picking a healthy turtle to begin with, make sure that you stay on top of their daily maintenance and upkeep to keep down any chances of illness or disease striking.

What are the Pros and Cons of Keeping Box Turtles?

In order to make a sound decision on whether or not a Box Turtle is the right pet for you, this section presents the pros and cons of keeping Box Turtles as pets. Hopefully, this will enable you to objectively balance your admiration and passion for these fascinating creatures with the reality of their care and maintenance.

Pros for the Box Turtle

- Fascinating, beautiful and amazing creatures – gentle, intelligent reptiles unique for being the only creature on earth that carries its home around with it to the extent that the turtle does!
- Aside from possible medical bills for unforeseen emergencies, and aside from the startup costs of setting up your pet's home, the cost of the upkeep of a Box Turtle is not that expensive as compared to other pets.
- Small, quiet, intelligent pets that stay contained within their enclosures.
- A good starting pet for those who are just starting to learn about keeping turtles or tortoises for pets. Compared to other species, Box Turtles are cheaper and a lot easier to feed.

- Once the details of housing, feeding, temperatures and care are taken care of – they make wonderful pets, especially if you are truly fond of turtles.
- Certain species like the Common Box Turtles are common enough that they are easy to find or locate and will not be expensive to purchase. You will also have to do your research on the legality of keeping them as pets in your area – some states or regions restrict or prohibit outright the keeping of certain turtle species as pets.

Cons for the Box Turtle

- Box Turtles, like most turtles, are high maintenance pets. They require particular care, especially in the daily upkeep and maintenance of their environmental habitat in terms of cleanliness, humidity, and temperature levels. This is not a pet you can leave alone for long, and neither is it a pet that you can ask just anyone to look after should you be gone for an extended period of time. If you cannot provide this kind of regular care, then this is probably not the best pet for you.
- It may not be easy to find a vet that specializes in Turtle care – but this is a must if you intend to bring one home as your pet.

- Turtles need lots of space – possibly both indoor and outdoor enclosures, depending on your turtle's particular needs.

- This is not a pet you can bring home on a whim – they can live for decades – up to 45 years, which means that your care and dedication to their care and maintenance must also be long-term, including their care in the eventuality that they may outlive you.

- Reptiles like the Box Turtles can be carriers of bacteria that is lethal to humans, such as Salmonella. This is not a good pet to keep in the same environment as small children, people with low immunity, or even other pets such as cats or dogs.

- Despite the relatively low costs, the time and energy investment in your turtle's care and maintenance can be considerable. Feeding Box Turtles also requires a well-balanced diet of protein and plants. That means you will be feeding them worms, cockroaches, snails, crickets, and other protein sources at some point – so this is not a pet to keep for the squeamish.

- This is not a very interactive pet and will not appreciate being cuddled or handled too much – a bit boring if you're looking for a more exciting pet.

Chapter Three: Purchasing Your Box Turtle

After having done your research and considered the various pros and cons of keeping Box Turtles as pets, if you can still honestly say that you are fully capable of taking care of one - the next step is figuring out where to get one.

The source of your Box Turtle is important because for one thing, commercial pet trades that deal with turtles caught from the wild are illegal. You cannot simply catch one from the wild and bring them home to keep as pets, and supporting those who do this by purchasing the turtles they sell is not a good idea. Despite our love and admiration for these creatures that make us want to bring them home for keeps, the most important thing is to ensure their continued survival in their natural environment – not in captivity, and in sufficient numbers.

Your best option is probably purchasing one from a reputable breeder. While pet stores may offer Box Turtles for sale, you will want to get healthy turtles that have had some socialization with humans – something a bit unlikely for turtles kept in commercial pet stores. Getting your turtle from a reputable breeder also ensure that you can be acquainted with the turtle's history, their parentage, their peculiarities, age, and other pertinent information to better prepare you for their eventual care.

On Adopting Rescues

When getting a new pet, adopting should always be considered before purchasing one. There are plenty of pets out there – turtles included – that need good homes. Adopting a rescued turtle can help save that turtle's life, and you will be doing your part in ensuring the continued wellbeing and existence of this species.

Sadly, many of the turtles that eventually wind up in rescues once belonged to owners who were no longer able to care for their pets. This is yet another example of why it is important to consider carefully all the possible repercussions before you bring one of these turtles home. If you cannot care for them the way they need to be card for – you will either wind up with a dead turtle, or end up surrendering one to a shelter yourself.

Be aware that rescues will want to screen potential owners of the turtles they offer up for adoption, so it's best to look at their site and check out their requirements. You'll probably agree that having the requirements for adoption posted upfront is both smart and responsible – both for the potential owner and the rescue. This prevents the possibility of adopted turtles from once more finding themselves homeless, abandoned or surrendered because the new owners did not know what they were getting into.

It is probably best to look for a rescue nearest your area to facilitate visiting and consultations. Here is a list of a few rescues to check out:

Reptile Rescue Center.
<http://www.reptilerescuecenter.org/requirements-by-species/box-turtles/>

Turtle Rescue League.
<http://www.turtlerescueleague.com/pet-turtles/turtle-adoption>

TurtleTails.com.
<http://turtle_tails.tripod.com/adoptions/adoptions_and_mo re.htm>

Gulf Coast Turtle and Tortoise Society Adoption Program.
<http://www.gctts.org/adoption>

Central Texas Tortoise Rescue Adopt a Tortoise.
<https://texastortoiserescue.com/adopt-a-tortoise/>

How to Choose a Reputable Box Turtle Breeder

You want to do the responsible thing and purchase your Box Turtle from a reputable breeder, but this may not always be so easy. For one thing, your first contact with the breeder may be at a distance, or online, and there is no way that you can verify or even see the turtle beforehand, or before the purchase. How do you even know you're getting a healthy Box Turtle that has been legally bred in captivity, and not caught from the wild?

Here are a few red flags that should alert you to be careful in dealing with someone selling Box Turtles – or to avoid them altogether:

- If their selling price is too cheap. It takes a long term investment of money, time and commitment to breed Box Turtles in captivity, so you can expect the breeder to price their turtles at a slightly reasonable price. If you come across someone selling Box Turtles for a very cheap price, however, or who is selling Box

Turtles in bulk, then you should probably look elsewhere. Even the most professional breeders will have difficulty raising more than a few hatchlings at a time, and certainly not for selling in bulk at the cheapest price they can get!

- Look at the turtle's size. It is illegal to sell turtles that are under 4 inches carapace length in the United States. Professional and reputable breeders know this as a matter of course. If they still offer hatchlings for sale despite this law, they may not know as much as they claim to know about the creatures they are selling.

- Reputable breeders and dealers care about their turtles beyond the potential profit that a sale could bring them. This means they are knowledgeable about the turtles they are selling, the turtle's history, the best way to care for them, and details about how they were bred. Should there be "deficiencies" in a turtle – such as pyramiding in the shells, etc., they will freely admit these details, too. You can probably tell who is a reputable breeder by simple observation and a well-informed and friendly conversation.

It is best to network a bit before picking out a breeder of your choice. Ask around, especially among people who keep Box Turtles of their own, and find out where they purchased their turtles. People will not hesitate to recommend a good breeder, and neither will they hesitate to give a frank opinion of breeders whose reputations are a bit shady. If you can find more than a few individuals who are fully satisfied with Box Turtles bought from a specific breeder, you should probably explore the leads they throw your way.

Tips for Selecting a Healthy Box Turtle

Naturally, you would want to be select a healthy Box Turtle if at all possible – but this may not be so easy. For one thing, it isn't always easy to tell what a turtle might be thinking or feeling if all they do is stare back at you or hide from you. And unlike most mammal pets, they don't whine, complain, cry, or have noticeable fevers. So how can you tell if that cold-blooded reptile you are bringing home is in the best shape possible?

First of all, look at the enclosure where it is being kept. This should be roomy, clean, and well-provided with food, water, sufficient substrate, hiding and basking places, and light and heat sources. Remember that turtles do not tolerate a change of environments very well, so where you see them is probably where they are currently living. And their immediate environment goes a long way in determining their state of health.

As for the turtle itself, watch out for the following warning signs of possible health conditions in the turtle:

- Lumps or redness anywhere on the skin, especially the head, eyes, nostrils, skin, and legs.
- Check out the turtle's skin, and be wary of cuts or injuries which could be potential egg laying sites for flies.
- The eyes should be open and bright, with no visible discharge from the eyes or mouth.
- The turtle's shell should be solid and firm, with the turtle having a solid weight as you lift it. Beware of any soft of moist spots on the shell. Pyramiding on the shell is common among captive-bred turtles, and is not necessarily a sign of ill health or abnormal growth and development.
- There should be no fungal growth inside the turtle's mouth, and its tongue should be a healthy pink.
- Finally, see if you can examine any of its feces which may be lying around. This should be firm, without signs of worms or egg masses in the turtle's stool.

Chapter Four: Caring for Your New Box Turtle

Caring effectively for your Box Turtle entails a thorough knowledge and understanding of the behavior of reptiles as a whole, and Box Turtles in particular. Primary to the care of Box Turtles is approximating their natural habitat as closely as possible – and this depends to a large extent on the type of Box Turtle you are dealing with and their region of origin. Eastern Box Turtles, for instance, belong to woodland areas while Ornate Box Turtles hail from arid and dry climates.

It is also important to understand that Box Turtles can be territorial – or at least, they develop a deep attachment to their home. This is why it is so important to understand what is entailed in providing them a proper home – the peculiar details of doing so, and the importance of regular maintenance. Many owners who end up giving up their Turtle do so because they were not able to factor in the costs and labor that goes into caring for a turtle before bringing one home. While some of these owners do surrender their pet turtles to rescues, others simply release their Box Turtles into the wild. This is sheer irresponsibility. Not only are you causing your turtle extreme stress by throwing him completely into a new and strange environment, you are also endangering the unique balance of the local ecology by introducing a new wildlife – and the repercussions are usually never good.

The Basics of Reptile Thermoregulation

As with most reptiles, Box Turtles are considered ectotherms – which means that their internal temperature depends on their ambient environment. For the Box Turtle to effectively regulate their temperatures, therefore, they must be able to move around in areas with varying temperatures within their enclosure – whether in hiding places or shade, in shallow water dishes to hydrate, or to bask in order to dry out. This is a behavioral adaptation of most reptiles and other ectotherms to help them regulate their body temperature. This is why it is so important to provide them with a fully equipped and well-designed enclosure.

Much of the turtle's activity, therefore, is dependent on the seasons and the movement of the sun, and on the external environment. In general, their period of greatest activity is during rainy weather, and also before dawn. By the time the sun is up in the sky, they would already have found a hiding place for the day. After brief periods of soaking in water, they also need time to bask in sunlight and dry off. Much of a Box Turtle's activities are geared towards helping it maintain moderate or temperate conditions for itself.

Box Turtle Housing or Enclosure

One of the first things you have to decide is whether you will be keeping your Box Turtle indoors or outdoors. Each requires careful thought, planning and preparation.

Outdoor enclosures can be good if your Box Turtle is native to your area or region. Many turtles do seem to be healthier and happier if they are kept outdoors, and nature itself will provide the temperature and sunlight requirements that your turtle needs. Even turtles kept indoors will occasionally have to be brought outdoors for sunlight exposure.

Outdoor enclosures should be surrounded by a fence that goes a good foot underground, and surrounded by a wire mesh top. Remember that Box Turtles are skilled diggers and climbers, and many owners have brought their turtles outdoors only to marvel at how quickly these slow moving creatures can suddenly disappear. Not only does effective fencing help keep your turtle confined, but it also keeps them protected against roving predators or even against the next-door neighbor's dog. In no instance should your turtle be allowed to freely wander outdoors.

On the other hand, indoor enclosures allow you to closely monitor your turtle's conditions, as well as control the temperature of its habitat. This is highly recommended particularly for Box Turtle pets when they are being kept in areas to which they are not endemic. This should be well-provided for with substrate that is made of a combination of potting soil, leaf mulch, and sphagnum moss. This holds humidity well, especially with regular misting.

Glass enclosures are not generally recommended for indoor housing. Many turtles will stubbornly try to get through the glass, and their inability to do so will cause them a whole lot of frustration and stress. On the other hand, the sight of much activity outside of their glass walls will keep them frightened, anxious and unable to relax.

Whether you are choosing indoor or outdoor enclosures, the area should be landscaped well to provide them with sufficient and interesting hiding places where they can lay low, hide, or seek privacy and protection. Half-logs, rocks, brush, or piles of leaves strategically placed should be present. A well-prepared hide box is also recommended. This can be made of any simple cardboard box in which your turtle can hide. Large, flat rocks which they can climb will also allow them the opportunity to file down their claws.

Finally, and the most important thing, is that your turtle's enclosure should be of sufficient size to allow them room for exploration. It's probably also a good idea to plant small shrubs that can provide both shade, humidity, and edible food sources such as strawberries.

Temperature and Lighting Requirements

A heating lamp should be provided to offer them warmth. Keep this to one side of the enclosure so that your turtle can move closer to it or farther away depending on its temperature needs. You should also provide your turtle with a hide box and several places or spots in the enclosure in which they can hide. Not only does this give them a chance to cool off should they need it, but turtles also do like their privacy – over and above that which they can get from retreating into their shells. The landscape of their enclosure should provide them with many interesting places to hide should they wish to do so.

Box Turtles need a good variety of temperatures within their enclosure so that they could regulate their temperature accordingly. Providing a ceramic heater in one area of the enclosure so that they could move closer or farther away from it as necessary is recommended, as well as the sufficient provision of cooler areas such as scattered shaded areas, a shallow water source where they can soak if necessary, and a basking area where they can dry off after soaking allows them sufficient room to regulate their internal temperatures accordingly.

Daytime temperature should be kept at around 68-72 degrees, with a basking area that has a maximum of 85 degrees. Overnight, temperatures should be brought down to around 60-75 degrees.

Box turtles need sunlight – or sufficient replacement for sunlight such as UV-B rays. A good lighting choice such as a full spectrum fluorescent lamp that provides at least 5% UVA/UVB lighting will also serve as a heat source, and this should be kept to one area of the enclosure and maintained at around 85 degrees. Occasionally, you should bring your turtle outdoors for a brief exposure to natural sunlight. Turtles that do not see sunlight for at least 12 hours each day can literally stop eating and become inactive. The lack of sufficient light and cooler temperatures could signal to them approaching winter months, thus making them prepare for hibernation. This should be avoided unless you are prepared to actually hibernate your Box Turtle.

Maintaining Humidity

Water is important to your Box Turtle. Their environment should be kept humid, and should be misted every so often to keep the humidity levels high. Keeping live plants in their enclosure will help maintain humidity levels, as well as approximate natural conditions as much as possible. Insufficient humidity, on the other hand, can cause various illnesses such as eye irritations and even respiratory illnesses. A Box Turtle's period of greatest activity is, in fact, just before dawn or at dusk when humidity levels are high, or during the rainy season. You'll probably notice that your turtle's appetite is greater after misting.

A ready dish of clean drinking water should be readily available. Soaking water prepared in a shallow dish should also be made available to them so that they can cool down, soak, and rehydrate from time to time. Turtles often defecate in water, so their water supply should be changed regularly to prevent the possibility of infection or contamination – and to keep your turtle's health at optimal conditions. Turtles kept in outdoor enclosures should be provided with an outdoor pond – and you will find them either swimming in this or just soaking at the shallow end for about an hour each day. Just make sure that these are kept at shallow levels to allow them easy egress, and to prevent the possibility of drowning.

Poor water sources are often the top causes of a pet turtle's ill health.

Chapter Five: Meeting Your Box Turtle's Nutritional Needs

It isn't enough to provide your Box Turtle with a spacious enclosure that is well-regulated and well-maintained. If you want to keep your Box Turtle healthy and thriving, you also have to provide them with a well-balanced diet.

Box Turtles can be a finicky lot to feed – and this can sometimes be worrying because many Box Turtles can suffer from chronic nutritional problems while in captivity. In the wild, they don't have the luxury of being picky about their food because of the natural seasonal changes they go through, and for this reason they are considered opportunistic eaters that eat pretty much whatever food they come across.

Such is no longer true for Turtles raised in captivity, and so poor nutrition is a very real danger. It is therefore extremely essential that you provide your turtle with a varied diet that provides them with as much of their nutritional needs as possible. Occasional variations can help entice even picky turtles to keep eating, but the nutritional value should always be present to help maintain your turtle's optimal health.

The Nutritional Needs of Box Turtles

Box Turtles are omnivores, which means that they eat both plants and animal-based foods. While they can eat just about anything, it is highly recommended that they be fed only foods that they would naturally come across in the wild – and that means avoiding artificial or man-made foods such as chips, hot dogs, cheese, bread, candy, etc. Doing so can only increase the fussiness of your turtle's choices in their food.

As a general guideline, their diet can be broken down as an equal 50% plant-based food, and 50% animal-based food. Depending on their life stage, however, this does vary somewhat. Box Turtles up to 4-6 years of age seem to primarily be carnivores, while adult Box Turtles tend to be more herbivorous. At all times, they should have easy access to clean and fresh drinking water. Please consult with your veterinarian regarding the best diet plan for your Box Turtle.

Animal or high-protein foods

You will probably want to explore a wide variety of protein-based food sources for your Box Turtle, which could include earthworms, caterpillars, mealworms, wax worms, wax worms, snails, slugs, moths, spiders, grasshoppers, crickets, beetles and even pinkies (or baby mice). Insects may not provide your turtle with enough calcium, so you will probably want to enrich their meal with calcium supplements such as powdered calcium carbonate, lactate, citrate, or gluconate. Dust the insect with these before feeding them to the turtle.

Occasionally, you might want to shake things up by giving them vitamin-fortified chows, but this should in no instance exceed 5% of the turtle's total diet. Commercial reptile pets can be an excellent source of protein, but it is always a good idea to offer them live food more often than food that is commercially bought. If you offer them dry feed or pellets, soak these in water for 30 minutes to soften them.

A word of warning regarding collecting various insects for food –avoid collecting them from your home garden as much as possible. It is preferential to collect them from the wild, to raise them yourself, or to buy them from pet stores, bait stores, or reptile breeders. This caution is to avoid collecting insects or slugs that have been exposed to fertilizers, insecticides or any other chemicals that may be harmful to your turtle.

Plant-based food, including fruits and vegetables

While plant-based food should comprise at least 50% of your Box Turtle's diet, you should offer them more vegetables than fruits – the latter should not be more than 10-20% of this portion. Fruits can entice your turtle's taste buds, but they can also be mineral deficient. On the other hand, they get more nutritional value from leafy greens so these should be fed more liberally.

Some of the fruits Box Turtles are fond of include strawberries, tomatoes, apples, grapes, cherries, pears, kiwi, oranges, figs, melons, bananas, mangoes, grapefruit, raspberries, peaches, pears, plums, and nectarines.

Dark, leafy green vegetables are highly recommended for Box Turtles, and these can include cabbage, spinach, romaine lettuce, broccoli, squash, sweet potatoes, carrots, beets, pea pods, and mushrooms.

Be careful when feeding your Box Turtle mushrooms – avoid toxic or the poisonous kind, especially if you are gathering many of your turtle's food from the wild.

Occasionally, you may wish to offer your turtle treats in the form of edible flowers such as carnations, dandelions, hibiscus, nasturtiums and geraniums.

Important Vitamins and Minerals

Vitamin A – Vitamin-rich foods include yellow or dark orange vegetables, dark and leafy green vegetables, and liver (for instance, from whole mice).

Vitamin D3 – This is usually sourced from sunlight or any other UVB producing light source. Vitamin D3 helps your Box Turtle in the conversion of calcium into usable compounds, and so most calcium supplements recommended for turtles also contain Vitamin D3.

Calcium – Turtles need a high dose of calcium, and many veterinarians recommend supplementing their dietary calcium with supplements. A light sprinkling of calcium powder (such as calcium gluconate, lactate, or carbonate) over their regular food can be done each week. Be careful, however, about over-supplementation. Always consult with your veterinarian before giving your turtle any supplement.

Fiber – Not getting enough fiber can be unhealthy for your turtle's digestive system, and that is why providing them with a healthy portion of leafy greens in their diet is important. In the wild, Box Turtles usually get their fiber from eating leaves and grasses.

Phosphorous – While Turtles to need phosphorous in their diet, this is already usually found in abundance in the usual foods they eat. It is highly recommended that any calcium supplements you provide your turtle should be those that do not contain phosphorous.

Water – Turtles need fresh, clean water at all times – not only for drinking, but also for soaking. Dehydration is a very real danger, especially for turtles kept in captivity, and regular misting is recommended, on top of the daily fresh supply of water. Offer your turtle its clean, fresh water in a clean, shallow dish or pan that will not be easily overturned, and with a kind of "ramp" along the sides so that your turtle can easily climb in and out of its own accord. Make sure that the water level does not reach higher than its chin, or else you are also running the risk of your turtle drowning. Box Turtles often defecate or pee in their water bowls, too – so it is imperative that their water dish should be cleaned regularly to avoid contamination or infections. Always to remember to wash your hands carefully after handling any of your turtle's equipment.

Tips for Feeding Your Box Turtle

One of the key ways of dealing with Box Turtles that are also finicky eaters is to provide them with as much variety as possible. Many suggest avoiding giving your Box Turtle the same food twice in a row – this can grow into an "addiction" or "fixation" for a particular food or taste, and can be very difficult to break later on.

- Box Turtles seem to be particularly attracted to red, yellow and orange foods. Also live, moving food can stimulate feeding. You can try cutting up or chopping fruits, vegetables and insects and mixing them together to better entice them to eat, while also providing them with a healthy and balanced meal.

- Feed your Box Turtle according to their natural daily rhythm. In the wild, turtles are most active during the early morning or late afternoon, when the sun is not too hot. Their activity also increases when it rains, so this is a good time to feed them when you are keeping them in an outdoor enclosure. If they are kept indoors, misting or spraying the cage with water can help stimulate their appetite.

- Wash the fruits and vegetables, then chop them into small, bite-sized pieces for easier feeding. Greater variety in the foods you feed your turtle can help ensure a healthy and balanced diet. Offer these to your turtle in a shallow dish that will not be easily overturned. Occasionally, you may wish to offer them their food on top of a flat rock which they can easily climb. This more natural approach will also help maintain their beaks and toenails from becoming overgrown.

- Feed adults three or more times per week, or every other day, in the morning. Juveniles and growing turtles should be fed daily.

- If you are keeping your turtle indoors, occasionally bringing them out for exposure to real sunlight may help improve their appetite.

- You can also try some variety in where you feed them if you are having a difficult time getting them to eat – some turtles do prefer a bit more privacy while feeding, so offering them food in a more sheltered area may be more enticing for them than right out in the open.

- If you find your turtle fixating on a particular food while also refusing to eat anything else, try mixing up their fave with the new food, chopping each finely to encourage them not to discriminate too much.

- If your turtle refuses to eat for more than two weeks, seek veterinary care. Sometimes their refusal to eat can be caused by a medical problem or eating disorder.

Chapter Six: Box Turtle Care and Husbandry

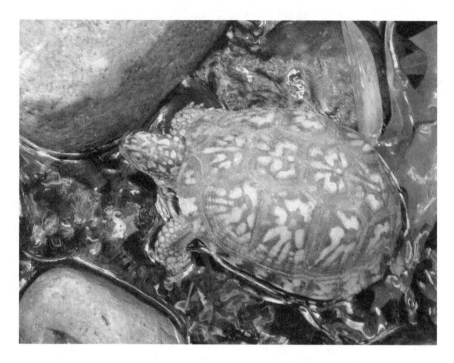

One of the keys to caring for your Box Turtle is learning as much as you can about their life and their behavior in the wild, and approximating this as closely as possible even in captive conditions. This entails doing a lot of independent research – focusing particularly on the type of Box Turtle you are, or are planning on, keeping. Naturally, the specific needs of each turtle changes depending on the type – which is essentially based on their region of origin. This means also learning as much as you can about the natural seasons, weather, climate, flora and fauna of your turtle's native region.

Understanding Box Turtle Behavior

Box Turtles are not an aquatic species – they spend most of their time on land, but they do need to soak in water from time to time. Overall, this is a gentle and friendly species, but one should never underestimate their wild instincts – and they will bite should they feel threatened. Most are pretty docile and it is generally safe to pick them up, but avoid handling them or picking them up too often. Turtles are not fond of being handled too much, and they can lash out if stressed. Much of the stress that captive Box Turtles experience in conditions of captivity include: drastic changes in the environment and improper or poor captive conditions.

Box Turtles are so called because of their distinctive behavior of retracting inside their shell and completely closing up using the movable hinge on their lower shell. No flesh is left exposed when this happens, and the Box Turtle has literally "boxed itself up" – usually in response to one form of perceived threat or another. In general, Box Turtles would far prefer retreating into their shell to protect themselves rather than aggressively biting or lashing out against threats.

It is never recommended for young children to handle Box Turtles – or if they should do so, the children should be closely supervised to ensure that no harm is caused to either child or turtle. Children can often be brusque in their handling of small creatures, and they can end up harming the turtle. Box Turtles are living, breathing creatures – they are not toys, and their temperament does not really necessitate a need for games or "play."

On the other hand, you should also ensure that children do not engage in unsafe practices such as kissing a turtle or putting their hands or fingers to their mouths after handling one. Proper hygiene should always be practiced around turtles in order to keep down the chances of transmission of bacteria that can be harmful to humans.

Box Turtle Hibernation or Brumation

Also depending on their region of origin and the seasons, Box Turtles are known for hibernating during the winter months – a process that is also sometimes referred to as brumation. This can last for 3-5 months, depending on the prevailing weather conditions. In regions where there is no true winter, Box Turtles may only slow down during the cooler winter months and not enter a true hibernation state at all.

Hibernation itself is triggered by a decrease in daylight hours and lowering temperatures. During these colder months and severe decrease in temperatures, given their dependence on external factors for internal temperature regulation, these adaptable turtles will dig in deep into the soil or substrate, looking for safer temperatures where they can maintain themselves in extreme conditions. Hibernating Turtles in the wild are essentially unprotected, and many can die during this period – whether due to harsh weather conditions or because they have become vulnerable to predators.

It is interesting to note that brumating or hibernating reptiles or Box Turtles also require this period to prepare for breeding – during this cooling period, ovulation is stimulated, as well as the production of sperm. Unless you are fully intending on breeding your Box Turtle, therefore, you might want to keep your turtles carefully separated when they come out of hibernation during the spring months, or you might find yourself responsible for a nest of eggs that will soon be living, thriving hatchlings!

Because hibernation or brumation is essentially dependent on external environmental conditions, many Box Turtle owners deliberate each time during the winter months whether or not they should even hibernate their turtle at all. Box Turtles living in captive conditions are essentially also living in artificial conditions, which means that outdoor seasonal changes need not affect your Box

Turtle too much. In certain instances, it may not be advisable to hibernate your Box turtle – for instance, if you have not had your Box Turtle for more than a year, when their health is in a poor condition, or when you do not have access to, or have not been able to prepare, a proper hibernation place for your turtle (a particular concern for turtles kept in outdoor enclosures).

On the other hand, hibernation or brumation is an essential part of a Box Turtle's growth and development – this helps them maintain normal thyroid activities and complete normal life expectancies. And of course, hibernation helps them synchronize their reproduction cycles and prepare for breeding and reproduction. But this can also be a dangerous time for the turtle – this is a period of time when the turtle's biological processes are barely working to keep them alive, including their immune system. An inappropriately chosen place for hibernation could also endanger them – whether due to flooding and eventual drowning, dehydration, freezing to death, or becoming vulnerable to predators.

A good rule of thumb is not to hibernate if your veterinarian finds something wrong with your turtle health-wise.

Preparing a Hibernaculum

In the wild, Box Turtles hibernate at temperatures below 50ºF, and hibernation periods generally begin at around mid-October. If you want your turtle to hibernate outdoors, you should prepare for them a safe and protected place where they can burrow into during the winter months – preferably under a mound of leaves or other protective covers such as logs or rocks. The ground should be prepared so that they could go as deeply as they need to go – some have been found to burrow to depths of at least 2 feet. You can then protect them from the possibility of drowning by protecting this area from rain or flooding by providing a water proof cover. You should, however, make sure that they have ready access to clean drinking water in case they should surface for a drink. Please remember that the turtles are very defenseless during this time, which means that unless you can guarantee their protection against roaming predators and other natural dangers, you should probably prepare an indoor hibernaculum for them instead, or simply not have them hibernate at all.

Box Turtles that are kept primarily indoors throughout the year might require a bit more preparation for brumation – ceasing to feed them 2-3 weeks prior to hibernation will alert their bodies to the natural food scarcity that takes place during winter. Allowing them to soak in tepid water will keep them hydrated and will also encourage elimination. This is important because undigested food left in their system can cause them severe illnesses over the next few months. Feed them high-fiber foods prior to this time to promote elimination.

Then begin to bring down the temperature in their enclosure by increments of some 5 degrees each time to allow it to acclimate to cooler temperatures. It is best to bring them to a vet for a checkup to ensure that its physical health is sufficient to carry it through hibernation conditions. Some owners use the refrigeration method to help mimic natural conditions of lower winter temperatures – the important thing is not to completely close or seal up the fridge door so as to maintain oxygen and breathing requirements.

If you do wish for your Box Turtle to hibernate indoors, prepare a suitable place for them to do so. This is called a hibernaculum or a hibernation box, and is the preferred method for turtles hibernating in areas to which they are not endemic, and for owners who wish to have greater control over the external conditions of their turtle's brumation.

Prepare a box or container and fill this with moist peat moss and newspaper. You can either leave this uncovered or place a lid on it with appropriately drilled holes. Once your turtle begins to slow down, place it into the smaller box and keep it in an area with a steady temperature ranging from 45-50ºF in a draft-free room. Humidity levels should also be maintained. Be sure to set aside clean water for your turtle in case it surfaces for a drink. Even for indoor hibernation boxes, you should ensure that your turtle will be kept safe from the dangers of foraging creatures, including Fire Ants.

Check up on your hibernating turtle periodically during the next 2-3 months – make sure that your turtle is properly hydrated, looks healthy, and is still hibernating. The substrate should be clean and free of molds – change it if necessary, or hydrate it again if it has become too dry. If your turtle has already become too active, or wakes up too often to look for a drink, it's possible that it may be sick. If so, you should bring it out of hibernation early and allow it to overwinter indoors. This entails gradually bringing up their core body temperature, regular feeding, and keeping it in warm and high humidity conditions.

To bring your turtle out of hibernation, the temperature should be incrementally increased – to 60ºF degrees for around two days, then to room temperature, then to their normal environmental conditions. Soak them every other day, and begin feeding them around two days after they have been returned to normal room temperatures. Be aware, though, that some turtles may not eat for some time – and certain males may not eat at all until after breeding.

Chapter Seven: Box Turtle Handling and Temperament

Many Box Turtle hobbyists and keepers will be quick to tell you that keeping one for a pet can be incredibly boring. You feed your turtle, you clean up after them, make sure they are safe and healthy and have everything they need, and they hardly demonstrate any affection or gratitude for all your efforts. Some days, you might not even catch a glimpse of them if they're feeling particularly private. Does that seem contrary to everything that a pet is supposed to be? Like with most reptiles, one should come to terms with the fact that Box Turtles make beautiful but rather indifferent pets – quite different from their portrayal in cartoons and animated movies or films.

Still, keeping one for a pet involves the occasional physical contact with your Box Turtle. It bears stressing that excessive handling can cause your pet turtle undue stress, and should be avoided when it is unnecessary to handle them in the first place. If you really do need to pick them up and handle them, for instance when you are checking their physical health, preparing to bring them to a vet, or need to move them so that you can give their enclosure a thorough cleaning, there are a few crucial things you need to remember.

Box Turtle Temperament

Box Turtles are attractive, fairly hardy, and intelligent animals. The temperament varies individually and by type, but in general, Box Turtles are gentle and mellow creatures. Their name derives from their ability to retract completely within their shell, using the hinged plastron on their carapace so that they can completely box themselves up within their shell. They typically grow to a moderate size of 4-7 inches, and live for approximately 40-50 years. They make great first time turtle pets, although they are still considered high maintenance pets.

If you are considering bringing home a Box Turtle as a pet, please do extensive research beforehand to make sure that you are capable of giving them the long term care that they need. And it is advisable to purchase or adopt only Box Turtles that have been bred in captivity, rather than those captured from the wild. The latter may be illegal in certain states, and turtles that have lived and survived in the wild can become extremely stressed when thrown into a new and strange environment. Box Turtles are known for being attached to their region of origin, and they do not like being transplanted completely into strange new surroundings. Doing so may only severely shorten their lifespan. Not to mention the fact that wild caught Box Turtles may carry parasites or bacteria with it that can be extremely harmful to humans.

Of course, even Box Turtles raised and bred in captivity have the same attachment to familiar surroundings, and they will also suffer stress and anxiety when thrown into a completely new environment – regardless of how beautiful the enclosure you prepared for it is. Box Turtles bred in captivity have been known to be more gentle in temperament, and are at least more familiar with the comings and goings of humans in their immediate surroundings.

Box Turtles are fairly hardy, but they can also be pretty delicate in terms of their constitution. As long as you provide them with a well-maintained and clean enclosure, and provide them a fresh supply of clean water and a well-balanced diet, illnesses and sicknesses can be kept to a minimum. It is always a good idea, however, to research the local vets in your area and find one that has experience in dealing with reptiles so that you know where to go in case of a medical emergency.

Tips for Handling your Box Turtle

Caution in handling your Box Turtle serves two purposes: it prevents you from causing your pet turtle any injury or undue stress, and also protects you from being attacked by your turtle (yes, it can happen), or from being affected by any dangerous bacteria or diseases that Box Turtles may carry.

Always remember to wash your hands thoroughly after handling your Box Turtle or any of their equipment such as their cage, dishes, or any of the plants, rocks, substratum, and other components of their enclosure. Doing so can help prevent the possibility of disease transmissions from any bacteria that your pet turtle may be carrying.

Many Box Turtles grown and raised in captivity can become responsive to the presence of their keepers – though this is probably because they are equating your presence to that of being fed. Unlike turtles in the wild that shy away from human contact, some acclimated turtles will eagerly position themselves to meet you when you come and feed them.

In general, however, Box Turtles do not like being handled, and even tame ones react negatively to being picked up and raised off of the ground. While this may sometimes be necessary during routine cage maintenance, for example, such handling should be kept to a minimum if at all possible. And Box Turtles should not be handled by children or persons with low immunity – if this cannot be avoided, there should be very close supervision.

Smaller turtles can be lifted with the fingers and thumb, and lifted by placing them on your open palm. They should always be restrained, however, in order to prevent their scrambling off and possibly injuring himself by a fall. Larger Box Turtles, on the other hand, should be grasped by both hands, one hand on each side of its shell. Be careful because some of them may react strongly by kicking or scratching. Try not to cause your turtle any scratches or injure its shell. Any injury they suffer, whether on their shell or otherwise, could possibly become infected. Remember that the turtle's shell is also a living and growing part of your turtle's physical makeup, and is not impervious to feeling. If you do get scratched yourself, the wounds should be siterilized before being dressed.

Needless to say, always take pains to ensure that you do not drop your turtle. This can cause them severe injury for which a vet's services should be sought immediately.

The Growth and Development of Box Turtles

A Box Turtle's skin is not like the skin of humans or animals which stretch and grow to accommodate one's growth. His skin is more leathery, tough, and may look like it is covered by small scales. Periodically, he will outgrow his skin, and as he does so, he sheds the old skin and leaves it behind. This is also true for their shell, in order to allow for their growth in size. But they also do this in order to prevent potential health risks such as infections that can come from shell rot or other parasitic infections that may have taken hold on its shell.

A turtle's body is covered by skin, and a shell that is made mostly of bone. This shell is fused to his body, and its outside is layered in plates or scales that are called scutes that cover and protect the bones and cartilage of the shell underneath. Scutes are akin to fingernails, and are made of the same substance called keratin.

Your turtle will occasionally shed its skin, but it will shed its scutes more often. When this happens, the scutes peel or flake off piece by piece and are replaced by new ones.

Turtles will shed when needed in order to prevent shell rot and infection – and this can happen if the turtle has soaked for too long in water, and is unable to dry themselves off effectively. These conditions are potential risks for shell rot. But in general, Box Turtles shed immediately before, and immediately after hibernation. Some peeling may be evident right before your Box Turtle hibernates, but the real and extensive shedding will occur right after it emerges from hibernation, during which you might find it basking more often. This is completely natural and promotes both healing and growth.

Signs that your turtle's shell is peeling in a healthy way are:

- Peeling scutes that are partially translucent and not too thick. These should look like the shell that they just came off of.
- The peeling scutes will look like they are "lifting up" off the shell, and will generally come off on their own. Please do not try to physically force or remove the scutes yourself.
- The scutes should be intact and whole, not coming off in parts.

Behavioral Characteristics of Box Turtles

Box Turtles are semi-terrestrial turtles that spend most of their time on land, and prefer to have a nearby source of water. Occasionally, they will soak in water and defecate in water, too. They do not, however, swim very well so that their soaking water should only be shallow and cleaned regularly to prevent contamination and infection from bacteria. It is therefore not advisable to house them in a water tank, or to provide them with a too-deep water bowl or dish in which they can possibly drown. Efficient water hygiene should be maintained – whether through water filtration or through simple daily changing of their water and regular cleaning of their water and food dishes.

Box Turtles come from a temperate climate, and their habitat usually consists of varying micro-environments with different temperatures and humidity levels among which they can move in order to regulate their body temperatures. Dehydration is a very real danger to them, so aside from plenty of shaded spots where they can take shelter from the sun, substrate deep enough that they can burrow into, readily available clean drinking water and a shallow water dish in which they can soak, they also need moderate levels of humidity in their environment. If you are keeping them in an indoor enclosure, it is best that this be equipped with substrate and plants that can help maintain humidity levels.

Occasionally, you should mist the cage using clean, sprayed water.

Box Turtles are often shy and prefer privacy, but they can also be aggressive and territorial – particularly when you find different males in the same environment. For this reason, it is advisable to keep each Box Turtle in their own separate enclosures. Not only does this prevent aggression and violence between different turtles, it also prevents unforeseen breeding and keeps down the chances of one sick turtle contaminating the rest.

Chapter Eight: Breeding Your Box Turtle

Mating between Box Turtles usually takes place throughout the spring and summer – after they come out of hibernation in March or early April. If you are keeping both a male and a female Box turtle as pets, then the possibility of their mating and breeding should be a reality you are aware of. If you do not wish them to breed, then you should do the responsible thing and keep them separate. Too many times, owners are just surprised when they see hatchlings emerging, not knowing how or when it happened. Like the breeding of most other pets, the breeding of Box Turtles should be handled responsibly by the owners. The first consideration should always be the health, maturity, and suitability of the breeding pair.

Remember that breeding, egg formation and laying can consume much energy for both the male and the female. They should be of sufficient age, maturity and state of health to be able to undertake this task well. If at all possible, neither should they suffer from any illnesses or deformities that would make their breeding more difficult, or perhaps compromise the health and wellbeing of the offspring. Most breeders also recommend against the breeding of two related turtles because their offspring could suffer from weakness, deformities, or early death.

If you do wish to breed your turtles, you should be responsible enough to think of the long-term results, including the care of the breeding pair and prospective parents, the care of the eggs and the hatchlings, and whether or not you will be able to find good homes for them later on. Be aware that certain states have laws against releasing captive bred turtles into the wild.

Selection and Care of the Breeding Pair

Sexing turtles is not that complicated. The males are usually more brilliant in coloring, while females have duller coloring. Males are often smaller than the females, but they have larger and longer tails, and rear nails. The males also have a concave underside (plastron) to enable him to conform better to the female's shell as he mounts her. The female's plastron, on the other hand, is flat. Ideally, you should choose adult male and female Box turtles of approximately similar size – approximately between 5-6 inches of carapace length, and between 7-10 years or age.

The female's fertility is largely dependent on her state of health – based on such general things as her diet and proper nutrition and being kept in a clean and low-stress environment. Keeping them in an outdoor enclosure will allow them to follow the natural seasonal changes to induce hibernation and turtle mating behavior, although some breeders do manage to induce these in indoor enclosures through the Refrigeration Method, which entails the preparation of a hibernacula kept at optimal temperatures. Either way, you should be able to check periodically on your turtle to make sure that they are kept safe, well insulated, and well-hydrated throughout their hibernation period. This natural process is often sufficient to induce turtle mating behavior.

The turtles should be in optimal health prior to hibernation – which could take place for at least two months.

Around spring or summer, as the turtles come out of hibernation, the males will have a strong urge to find a mate. You will probably observe some displays of their courtship ritual, including males circling the female, butting against her, and sometimes even biting her. Some males can often be quite aggressive, and will even try to bite the female's head and front legs when he mounts her. This is why it is so important to select turtles appropriately sized to each other.

The mating process itself is also pretty straightforward. When the female lowers her plastron, the male is then able to hook his feet beneath her carapace and they begin copulating. The female will lock up her carapace so that the male doesn't not slide off during copulation - which can take place for about an hour or so.

The female's nesting and laying of the eggs will take place around the warmer months of June or July, during which time you should have already provided your female with a solitary pen with a nesting site – ideally several choices of nesting sites among which she can make her selection. You can do this by providing rocks or large tree branches for cover, and a moist mix of sand and soft top soil that is about 8 to 12 inches deep. This pen should be equipped in the same way that a turtle's main enclosure is equipped. The goal is to provide your female the feeling of security and some privacy while also ensuring her optimal health and care.

Laying and Care of the Eggs

Around the time that the female is ready to lay her eggs, she will begin looking for an appropriate nesting spot. She will likely prefer a protected and private spot – usually near a tree limb or a rock She will engage in digging her egg chamber using her back feet for about several hours or until she has created a three-four inch deep receptacle for the eggs. Eggs usually average at 2-4, and are white, oval, with thin-walled and permeable shells. Once she is done laying the eggs, the female will cover them again with the soil she had displaced, packing the soil in place with her hind legs until you can hardly tell that the soil had been disturbed.

Eggs hatch approximately eighty days after being laid, but it could be difficult to pinpoint exactly when the eggs are actually laid. Females will bury the eggs after laying them, and it is strongly advised that you limit the checks on the enclosure because she would strongly prefer solitude at this time. And in fact, it is not advisable to disturb move turtle eggs once they have been laid. Make sure to check on her (as opposed to looking for eggs) regularly all the same – and don't be lax about changing her water, cleaning up her enclosure as best you could, and providing her with adequate food. Artificially incubating and hatching eggs requires expertise and experience – not to mention great expense, and is not something recommended for first time or novice turtle pet owners. If you do take the eggs away from the mother, it's quite likely that you won't produce any living hatchlings.

Care for the eggs will really be up to the mother after she has laid them, and your role in the process will be limited. Still, and particularly if your turtle is being kept in an outdoor enclosure, you might want to provide extra protection for the eggs. A wire mesh cover will help secure the eggs from other animals, including other turtles. It will also keep the hatchlings from escaping once they have hatched. While they will generally hatch around 80 days after being laid, the range of time can be anywhere from 70-90 days, depending on the prevailing temperature, which in turn determines how quickly the embryos will develop. If you find the soil or ground to be hard, you may want to water the ground around day 75. This helps the hatchlings dig their way out of the soil when they are ready to emerge.

If you find any eggs laid out in odd places – unburied, or in the water dish, for instance, these are most likely unfertile eggs which the mother has knowingly discarded for this very reason.

Caring for the Hatchlings

In the wild, the mortality rate of Box Turtle hatchlings are quite high. They are very susceptible to the elements, particularly in their first year, and they are considered prey by various animals such as rodents, ants, and raccoons. If the eggs have been kept in an outdoor enclosure until now, you might want to transfer them to an indoor enclosure during their first year. This is the time when it becomes important for you to exercise care and protection over the hatchlings.

If you wish to keep them in an outdoor enclosure instead, make sure to provide the hatchlings with all the necessary protection they will need against probable predators and the elements - overexposure to the sun or to the rain could kill them just as easily as a frenzy of Fire Ants that might get into the enclosure. Provide them with areas of shade and a hide box, and ant bait could be used to keep fire ants from getting into the pens and feeding on the baby turtles. Practicing regular maintenance by cleaning out uneaten food and getting rid of waste also helps ensure minimal chances of ant incursions and bacteria or germs affecting the hatchlings.

If you have decided to move your hatchlings indoors, it is advisable to keep the hatchlings in separate tanks. If you do not wish to do this, it is advised that you feed them separately, as they can be quite aggressive during feeding time. If they also display aggression against littermates even outside of feeding time, then separating them from each other better ensures their survival as a whole.

Their indoor tanks or enclosures usually consist of deep substrate which can be misted daily to maintain high humidity levels. Heat should be maintained at around 82°F during the day, and around 75°F at night. You can maintain the tank's temperatures using an overhead lamp of 40-60 watts and/or a low wattage thermostat or heater. You can monitor the tank's temperature by the use of thermometers attached to the tank in several locations. Clean the tank at least once or twice a month, depending on the conditions within the tank. Change the water daily, and make sure to clean or change beddings that contain the turtle's waste. Practicing good tank maintenance at this time will keep germs and bacteria at bay, and goes a long way in ensuring the good health and proper development and growth of your tiny Box Turtle.

Provide the hatchlings with a hide box where they can go if they wish to cool off a bit. You should also provide them with regularly changed fresh and clean water in a shallow dish. Bring them outdoors at least once a week, providing them with filtered sunlight for at least an hour each time. Even then, you should always provide the hatchlings with a shade or hiding place where they can retreat should the sun prove to be too intense for them. They should in no instance be left alone during this time. They could literally overheat under inappropriate conditions.

The recommended diet for a hatchling is one that is high in protein, at a ratio of around 80% protein and 20% plant matter. Small bugs, for instance, can give them much of their protein needs. Uneaten food should be cleaned out after an hour or these could attract bugs or insects, and possibly become the breeding ground of bacteria.

Exercise your best judgment in terms of caring for your hatchlings. This can consume much of your time and energy, but the difference in raising sick turtles to healthy ones make all that effort worthwhile. Be observant of the hatchlings in your care, and learn to make adjustments accordingly depending on your observations. And of course, keep reading and asking questions – educate yourself and read as much available materials as you can find.

Chapter Nine: Keeping Your Box Turtle Healthy

Box turtles of the genus *Terrapene* are fairly hardy animals – though their state of health does depend, to a large extent, on you as their owner and how you keep them. They require specific care, and can be stressed by over-handling or when being moved into new surroundings. On the other hand, they can also be prone to certain illnesses and conditions - and most of the time, these are brought on by poor advice. This is why it is important that you do your research prior to, and during, your ownership, of a pet Box turtle. In many cases, appropriate environmental and dietary maintenance will address these problems successfully.

And yet, despite our best efforts, sometimes our pets can just get sick from time to time. Below are some of the more common health problems of Box turtles and recommended treatments.

Common Conditions Affecting Box Turtles

Below we take a closer look at some of the common conditions that Box turtles are prone to. If you are planning on keeping a Box turtle for a pet, or already have one, do your research and find a good turtle vet in your area – preferably one that has experience in dealing with this particular species. In fact, if you suspect your Box turtle of being sick, or notice any deviation in their usual behavior, bring them to a vet immediately. Try not to undertake any homemade treatments until after you have sought professional care and treatment.

Common conditions that can affect Box Turtles include:

- Swollen and closed eyes

- Ear abscesses
- Parasites
- Shell and Skin Problems
- Respiratory Infection
- Metabolic Bone Disease

Swollen and Closed Eyes

Box turtles originate from temperate (not tropical) environments, and they will not tolerate extreme heat or dryness. If there is not enough moisture in their environment, eye infections can be quite common. You may notice that your turtle's eyes are shut and won't open unless he is soaked in warm water.

Another possible cause of eye infections is contaminated bathing or drinking water, or if its bedding is irritating to its eyes. Should the eyes be swollen enough that they become permanently closed, the turtle will not eat, thereby further compromising his health.

There are different ways by which you can maintain the humidity or moisture in your turtle's environment. Daily misting with water, readily available clean water that it can walk into any time it needs to, fixing a draft in the enclosure by which the turtle is drying out, substrate that is too absorbent and which is sucking the water right out of

Chapter Nine: Keeping Your Box Turtle Healthy

your pet, and placing plants in the enclosure, will help maintain the humidity in your turtle's environment. Cedar shavings or cedar bark are not recommended because these contains oils that are toxic to most reptiles. Bedding such as shredded paper or corncob bedding can also be considered too absorbent for your turtle's environment.

If the eyes look sunken it, it could be a sign of severe dehydration. If the eyes are closed and puffy, on the other hand, and you notice a discharge from the eyes or nostrils, it could be a sign of respiratory infection or vitamin A deficiency. Consult with your vet for proper diagnosis and treatment. Antibiotic eye ointment is usually quite effective in most cases.

Ear Abscesses

Ear abscesses is considered the number one health problem of captive Box turtles – and this condition is usually caused by the same conditions that cause swollen eyes, such as poor turtle care that involves dirty water or water that is too cold, too much or too little humidity, a poor diet, or respiratory illnesses. Any of these conditions can allow bacteria to enter and infect a turtle's body.

Box Turtles as Pets   P a g e | **88**

While a turtle might develop an abscess anywhere underneath their skin, they are particularly susceptible to middle ear infections which can result in an abscess that can appear as large bulges on either side of the head, or what looks like a big bump on the side of the head, in the same area where the ears are. An ear abscess means that there is a swelling of the Tympanic membrane, and a cyst develops underneath it, growing worse as the infection does. On the other hand, bacterial abscesses in places other than the ear are often caused by puncture wounds, bite wounds, and other injuries.

An ear abscess is very painful to your pet turtle, and requires professional treatment – an operation that requires either aspiration, or lancing, draining, and a lot of post-operative attention including antibiotics to kill off any remaining infection. It is also recommended that the site be left open to heal rather than being sutured after surgery, though taking care to keep the area clean and covered, and protected from attacks by flies, other insects and animals. Otherwise, recurrences might be common.

Parasites

Box turtles are semi-carnivorous, and so they are exposed to a wide range of parasites – as they eat many of the intermediate hosts. Practicing good and efficient hygiene will help keep the incidence of parasites down, but there will still be instances when your pet turtle might be attacked by either internal or external parasites. While all reptiles are prone to parasites, even in the wild, keeping them confined or in an enclosed space may increase the risks exponentially. That is why it is important to maintain the cleanliness of their surroundings – clean out fecal matter daily, and always clean out their water and food dishes. Needless to say, always wash your hands before and after handling any of your turtle's equipment.

Internal parasites are those which your turtle may ingest, such as worms (pinworms, hookworms, tape-worms, oxyurid and ascarid worms), protozoans that might be ingested when they eat contaminated foods or substrate, and other flagellate organisms. Possible signs and symptoms that may indicate that your turtle may have internal parasites include:

- Diarrhea
- Constipation
- Worms in the faeces
- Foaming mouth
- Regurgitating food
- Constipation
- Lethargy
- Lack of appetite

- Loss of weight
- Dark green and smelly urine
- Anorexia
- Fluid retention

Should you notice any of these symptoms, it is advisable to bring your turtle to a vet. Generally, analysis of a stool sample will tell your vet whether internal parasites are indeed the problem. Deworming meds are usually prescribed. It is important, however, that Ivermectin and Piperazine should not be used since these could be toxic to your turtle.

External parasites, on the other hand, can include pests such as ticks, leaches, mites, mosquitoes, fire ants, fly larvae, and chiggers. These can usually take hold of your pet when they are housed in an outdoor pen, or if you add decorations or substrate to their enclosure without cleaning them first.

Treatment depends on which parasite you are dealing with. Many pests can simply be picked off or removed with a pair of tweezers, such as mites, leaches, and ticks. An infestation of fire ants need to be addressed differently as these can kill your turtle by getting inside the shell once your pet tucks its head inside. The location of the ant nest should be located and exterminated if possible. Otherwise, bait traps can be laid so that the ants will not get inside your turtle's pen. Caution should always be exercised when dealing with chemicals of any kind, however – especially those which your pet turtle might also be exposed to.

On the other hand, open wounds or injuries are susceptible to the laying of fly eggs and larvae – when these hatch, they will feed on the flesh as they grow. You will need professional treatment should this happen. There will be a swelling or small lumps on the skin from which pupate will emerge and fall off. A vet will need to cut open this lump and clean out the wound.

In any case, it is always advisable to seek professional assistance or to consult with your veterinarian to help with the identification of the problem parasite, as well as the best way to remove any type of external or internal parasites. Proceeding recklessly will likely just worsen your turtle's condition.

Shell Rot

Also referred to as Septemic Cutaneous Ulcerative Disease (SCUD), this happens when an open wound or other injury becomes infected by a fungus or bacteria, or it can happen due to a filthy environment. Malnutrition can be a predisposing factor. When shell rot takes place, either the upper shell or the lower shell can suffer erosion. While this happens more often among aquatic turtles, this can also happen with land species like Box turtles.

The primary way of preventing shell rot is by keeping the turtle's enclosure clean. The build-up of fungus inside the confined space can usually be attributed to poor water quality. Soft, discolored shell which may or may not smell rotten is a sign of wet rot. Dry rot, on the other hand, is seen through a flaky, pitted shell with whitish patches.

It is imperative that you change your turtle's water often. This is true even if the water still seems clear and clean. Filters should be cleaned regularly using cool water. Faeces and all uneaten food should be removed as soon as possible. And your Box turtle should have a readily accessible dry area where it can bask and dry their shell when needed. The important thing is to minimize the possible places where bacteria or fungus can take hold and thrive.

If you suspect your Box turtle of having shell rot, bring him to your vet immediately. Shell rot needs to be treated immediately before it gets any worse, and your vet will work on removing the rotten parts while prescribing antibiotics to fight infection. Should their skin also be affected by the fungus, a salt bath for the next 4-5 days can help.

Afterwards, your turtle should be kept dry with only a limited time in the water each day. This keeps the infection from spreading. The short soaking time each day would keep your turtle from becoming dehydrated. Afterwards, the conditions which led to the rot in the first place needs to be addressed: regularly changed clean water, with a dry area where your turtle can bask and dry out their shell is important. Otherwise, shell rot can keep coming back. If it becomes a systemic infection, it can take a very long time to heal, not to mention that severe shell rot can eventually work its way into your turtle's blood and bone. The owner should be vigilant in preventing this from happening in the first place, or from recurring if it should happen.

Respiratory Infection

This is another possible result of poor environmental conditions – typically of enclosures that are kept too dry or too damp, sometimes too cold. Remember that Box turtles hail from a temperate environment. Poor care can cause a runny nose and swollen eyes, and they will not necessarily develop into an infection unless the condition is prolonged. When this happens, then the turtle's condition can worsen into an actual infection.

Some of the earlier signs that should alert you that something is wrong include open-mouthed breathing, mucous coming from the mouth, lack of appetite, and lethargy. When it becomes a full-blown infection, you'll notice your turtle swimming lopsided, breathing with a gaping motion or with raspy or wheezing sounds, and that they are basking more often than usual while at the same time showing difficulty breathing. Sometimes, you may even see discharges or bubbles forming from their nose or eyes.

Most vets will prescribe antibiotics, and this should do the trick – provided the conditions which led to the development of this condition in the first place is corrected. There should be sufficient moisture in your turtle's enclosure, with enough basking areas, regular cleaning and changing of the water, and avoiding drafts should keep down the chances of a recurrence.

Metabolic Bone Disease (MBD)

Metabolic Bone Disease or MBD, also sometimes called nutritional secondary hyperarathyroidism, is the result of a variety of ongoing environmental factors, including poor diet, lack of needed vitamins and minerals such as Vitamin D and a poor calcium and phosphorous ratio, lack of exercise, too much protein and fat, poor lighting, and low humidity.

When MBD strikes a young turtle, their growth and development is also compromised – and various deformities and poor body structure is the result: a soft or malformed shell and bones, stacked or raised scutes on the carapace, overgrown or parrot-like beaks, odd curvature in the nails, splayed legs, shells that curve upward like saddles, or thickened shells, thin and deformed legs. Because of the malformation of their legs and nails, they will also have difficulty walking.

MBD is the result of long-term exposure to poor conditions, and the best way to address it is through prevention: do your research properly on the proper housing conditions for your Box turtle. Provide them with a clean environment, a nutritious diet with a good supply of calcium and Vitamin D, appropriate lighting, plenty of exercise and the proper amounts of humidity.

This is a slow-growing condition, which means that it is not always easy to catch in the beginning. It is recommended that as soon as you notice any shell deformity, you should take a second look at their diet and living conditions to assess whether they are lacking in calcium, vitamin D, or exposure to full spectrum sunlight, that helps in the building of strong bones. Bring them to a vet for a professional diagnosis, and a consultation regarding changes you are planning on making. Make adjustments as are necessary. If this condition goes untreated for a long time, it will eventually result in the turtle's death.

Preventing Your Turtle from Becoming a Health Hazard

When it comes to health issues, it isn't just the health of your Box turtle that you have to take care of, but also your own health and the health of the rest of your family or household.

This is because reptiles such as the Box turtle can be carriers of bacteria that, while it may not make the turtle sick, can have a very different effect on humans. Reptiles, for instance, may carry salmonella which can cause salmonellosis in humans. This is a serious illness that can lead to diarrhea and vomiting in humans, and more severe symptoms in humans with compromised immune systems.

It is always best to practice good hygiene when dealing with pet animals. Below are some practical tips you can practice to help prevent any incidences of possible disease transmission from animals to humans:

- It is best to assume that your pet turtle carries the salmonella bacteria until after you've had him tested and cleared by a vet. Make this a yearly checkup with your vet to ensure your pet's continued good health and to check for possible illnesses, bacteria, or other diseases.

- Young children, particularly those younger than 5 years, and people with compromised immune systems are the ones most at risk. If they are part of your household, then perhaps a Box turtle is not the best pet for you to keep. If you already do have a Box turtle at home, the young children and those with compromised immune systems should not be allowed to touch your Box turtle.

- To help prevent the possible spread of bacteria or infection, always be meticulous in washing and cleaning your hands after handling your pet turtle, or any part of their tools, equipment, or habitat.

- Your Box turtle should not be allowed to roam freely in your house. If you use any household items or fixtures, like a sink or a tub to soak your turtle, be sure to disinfect the sink or tub afterwards. Never clean any of your turtle's equipment and items in or near places where you prepare food. Use outdoor wash pans and faucets as much as possible, and clean and disinfect these afterwards.

- Keep your turtle's enclosure or habitat clean, and make sure you dispose properly of any waste afterwards.
- If you are going to allow young kids to touch or handle the turtle, supervise the children closely. Make sure that they do not kiss the turtle or place their hands or fingers into their mouths. Afterwards, supervise the child as they wash their hands thoroughly.

Box Turtle Care Sheet

      Below is a quick summary of Box Turtle information – allowing you to see and appreciate Box Turtles at a glance. It is a ready-reference guide for those wishing to locate specific information about Box Turtles without having to read through the rest of this book, and it also allows you to easily refresh yourself about pertinent Box Turtle info that you may need at a moment's notice. For those still trying to decide whether or not a Box Turtle is the right pet for them, this section allows them a quick peek into this amazing creature and what caring for one would entail.

1.) Basic Box Turtle Information

Kingdom: Animalia

Phylum: Chordata

Class: Reptilia

Order: Testudines

Suborder: Cryptodira

Family: Emydidae

Genus: Terrapene

Species: Terrapene Carolina, Terrapene Coahuila, Terrapene Nelsoni, Terrapene Ornata

Regions of Origin:

- Common Box Turtles – South-Central, Eastern, and South Eastern parts of the United States, the Yucatan Peninsula and North Eastern parts of Mexico
- Ornate Box Turtle – South central and Southwestern parts of the United States, including adjacent parts of Mexico
- Spotted Box Turtle – North-Western Mexico
- Coahuilan Box Turtle – Cuatro Cienegas Basin in Coahuila, Mexico

Primary Habitat: Box Turtles occupy a wide variety of habitats depending on the type and region of origin, and can include grasslands, Mesic woodlands, semi-desert with occasional rainfall, or marshes

Description: Characterized by a domed shell with a hinged bottom. They don't have teeth, but have a rigid beak with upper and lower jaws covered by sharp, horny ridges which they use to eat tough and fibrous vegetation. Shell color patterns differ depending on the species, and helps them blend better into their environment. While the turtle's vertebra is rigid and elongated in the central part of the shell, it is small and flexible in the neck and tail, for easier movement.

Male irises are red or orange, and a female's is brown or yellow. But a better way to distinguish them by gender is the plastron, or the bottom shell. This is more concave in males for easier mating. Box Turtles have a hinged joint at the bottom which they can close tightly after hiding within its shell to serve as protection against predators.

Length: In general, adults range from 4-7 inches across the carapace, but there are still variations in size among the different species.

Weight: 1-2 lbs

Conservation Status:

- Common Box Turtles – Vulnerable
- Ornate Box Turtle – Near threatened

- Spotted Box Turtle – No official status due to lack of study
- Coahuilan Box Turtle – Endangered

Health Conditions: Swollen and closed eyes, Ear abscesses, Parasites, Shell and Skin Problems, Respiratory Infection, Metabolic Bone Disease

Lifespan: average 40-50 years

2.) Habitat Requirements

Recommended Equipment: Non-glass enclosure equipped with substrate that can hold moisture and is deep enough for them to burrow into; furnish with various natural items such as logs, rocks, tree bark, and other items that they can hide under or climb up on. Include a water bowl that is large enough for your turtle to soak in, but shallow enough that they can get out of it easily. Make sure that the water dish will not be easily upset by your turtle's weight.

Lighting and Heating Requirements: Provide sufficient light, warmth and UVB radiation, look for specialty bulbs sold in pet stores. Mount the bulb or bulbs some 12 to 16 inches above the substrate at one end of the enclosure so that your turtle can move closer or farther away from the heat and light source as needed. A digital thermometer will help you determine the proper temperature for your turtle's enclosure. Turn on the UV heat lamp some 12 hours each day, and then turn them off to approximate the day and night cycle

Recommended Temperature: 70-85 degrees Fahrenheit, while nighttime temperatures should not drop below 65 degrees.

Recommended Humidity Levels: Well-selected substrate or bedding and plants in the enclosure can help maintain humidity levels, as well as regular misting using a bottle.

Cleaning Frequency: Clean and change the water in the water bowl daily, with a more thorough cleaning 1-2 times a month, or more often if necessary

3.) Nutritional Needs

Nutritional Needs: Protein, Vegetables, calcium, Phosphorous, vitamin D3, Vitamin A; primary diet consists of 50% protein sources and 50% vegetable sources

Feeding Frequency (Adult): Every other day or 2-3 times per week

Feeding Frequency (Juvenile): Everyday

Water: Should be freely available at all times

4.) Breeding Information

Age of Sexual Maturity: around four years old, though full adult size is reached only around twenty years

Mating Season: Warmer months of March or April, after they come out of hibernation

Nesting Months: June or July

Clutch Size: average of 3-4 eggs

Incubation: Approximately 70-90 days

Recommended Incubation Temperatures and Humidity Levels: 84 degrees Fahrenheit, with misting every 2-3 days

Index

V

W

Y

Photo Credits

Page 1 Photo by Stevecrye via Wikimedia Commons. <https://commons.wikimedia.org/wiki/File:4-year-old-MaleTerrapeneOrnataLuteola.jpg>

Page 7 Photo by Onebiglie via Wikimedia Commons. <https://commons.wikimedia.org/wiki/File:Ornate_terrapin_hatchling.jpg>

Page 17_ Photo by Patrick Feller via Wikimedia Commons. <https://commons.wikimedia.org/wiki/File:Terrapene_ornata_ornata.jpg>

Page 33 Photo by Sue in az via Wikimedia Commons. <https://commons.wikimedia.org/wiki/File:Desert-box-turtle.jpg>

Page 41 Photo by Katja Schulz from Washington, D.C., USA via Wikimedia Commons. <https://commons.wikimedia.org/wiki/File:Common_Eastern_Box_Turtle_(14766043217).jpg>

Page 49 Photo by Stephen Friedt via Wikimedia Commons. <https://commons.wikimedia.org/wiki/File:Eastern_box_turtle_in_florida.JPG>

Page 57 Photo by Xxxsexxx via Wikimedia Commons. <https://commons.wikimedia.org/wiki/File:Box_turtle.jpg>

Page 65 Photo by Virginia State Parks staff via Wikimedia Commons.
<https://commons.wikimedia.org/wiki/File:BOX_TURTLE_1_(5853886646).jpg>

Page 75 Photo by Srs01 via Wikimedia Commons.
<https://commons.wikimedia.org/wiki/File:T._c._bauri_hatchling.jpg>

Page 85 Photo by U.S. Fish and Wildlife Service Headquarters via Wikimedia Commons.
<https://commons.wikimedia.org/wiki/File:Mattaponi_Wildlife_Management_Area,_Virginia_(7468016636).jpg>

Page 101 Photo by Lemos-Espinal J, Smith G via Wikimedia Commons.
<https://commons.wikimedia.org/wiki/File:Amphibians-and-reptiles-of-the-state-of-Coahuila-Mexico-with-comparison-with-adjoining-states-zookeys-593-117-g002.jpg>

References

"5 Interesting Facts About Common Box Turtles." Darren Poke. <https://haydensanimalfacts.com/2014/08/22/5-interesting-facts-about-common-box-turtles/>

"12 Reasons Not to Buy a Pet Turtle or Tortoise." Ben Zoltak. <https://pethelpful.com/reptiles-amphibians/10-Reason-Not-To-Buy-A-Pet-Turtle-Or-Tortoise>

"Adopt a Tortoise." Central Texas Tortoise Rescue. <https://texastortoiserescue.com/adopt-a-tortoise/>

"Adoption Requirements for Box Turtles." Reptile Rescue Center. <http://www.reptilerescuecenter.org/requirements-by-species/box-turtles/>

"Adoptions and More." TurtleTails.com. <http://turtle_tails.tripod.com/adoptions/adoptions_and_more.htm>

"Adoption Program." Gulf Coast Turtle and Tortoise Society. <http://www.gctts.org/adoption>

"Animals in Schools and Daycare Settings." CDC. <https://www.cdc.gov/features/animalsinschools/index.html>

"Are Turtles Expensive Pets?" Animal Questions. <http://animalquestions.org/reptiles/turtles/are-turtles-expensive-pets/>

"Asian Box Turtle." Wikipedia. <https://en.wikipedia.org/wiki/Asian_box_turtle>

"Ask the Vet: Turtles can make great pets with some TLC." Anne Pierce. <http://gazette.com/ask-the-vet-turtles-can-make-great-pets-with-some-tlc/article/89813>

"Avoiding Problems with Box Turtles." Tortoise Trust. <http://www.tortoisetrust.org/articles/avoidbox.html>

"Behavioral Observations." MC Biology Box Turtle Observation Project. <http://w3.marietta.edu/~mcshaffd/boxt/behavior.html>

"Box Turtle." Avian and Exotic Animal Care + Veterinary Hospital. <http://www.avianandexotic.com/care-sheets/reptiles/box-turtle/>

"Box Turtle." Regal Pet. <http://regalpet.com/pets/597-box-turtle>

"Box Turtle." Wikipedia. <https://en.wikipedia.org/wiki/Box_turtle#Conservation_status>

"Box Turtle Care." AAHA. <https://www.aaha.org/pet_owner/pet_health_library/other/general_health/box_turtle_care.aspx>

"Box Turtle Care." Box Turtles.
<http://www.boxturtles.com/box-turtle-care/>

"Box Turtle Care." Mary Hopson.
<http://turtlepuddle.org/american/boxcare.html>

"Box Turtle Hibernation: Pre and Post-Brumation Care." Pet
Education.
<http://www.peteducation.com/article.cfm?c=17+1797&aid
=3363>

"Box Turtle Illness Symptoms." Pets on Mom.Me.
<http://animals.mom.me/box-turtle-illness-symptoms-
2036.html>

"Box Turtle Mating." A Box Turtle.
<http://aboxturtle.com/mating.htm>

"Box Turtle: Pros and Cons." Yahoo Answers.
<https://answers.yahoo.com/question/index?qid=201212110
75728AAHSywn>

"Box Turtles." Box Turtles. <http://www.boxturtles.com>"

"Box Turtles as a Health Hazard." Box Turtle World.
<http://www.boxturtleworld.com/box-turtle-care/box-
turtles-as-health-hazard/>

"Breeders and Dealers: Green Lights and Red Flags." Steve
Enders and Anthony Pierloni.
<https://theturtleroom.com/blog/2012/06/22/breeders-and-
dealers-green-lights-and-red-flags/>

"Breeding Box Turtles." Box Turtles. <http://www.boxturtles.com/breeding-box-turtles/>

"Breeding Your Box Turtles." Box Turtle Care and Conservation. <http://boxturtlesite.info/breed.html>

"Buying a Box Turtle." Box Turtles. <http://www.boxturtles.com/buying-a-box-turtle/>

"Captive Reptile & Amphibian Permit/License." Maryland Department of Natural Resources. <http://dnr.maryland.gov/wildlife/Pages/Licenses/captive.aspx>

"Care of Box Turtles." California Turtle & Tortoise Club. <https://www.tortoise.org/general/boxcare.html>

"Chelonians: Wild Caught or Captive Bred?" Katrina Smith. <http://www.reptilesmagazine.com/Wild-Turtles-And-Tortoises/Chelonian-Wild-Caught-Captive-Bred/>

"Choosing a Turtle." My Turtle Cam. <http://www.myturtlecam.com/choose.php>

"Common Health Problems." Turtle Rescue of Long Island. <http://www.turtlerescues.com/common_health_problems.htm>

"Diet for Feeding Your Box Turtle." Dave Donovan. <http://small-pets.lovetoknow.com/diet-feeding-your-box-turtle>

"Ectotherm." Wikipedia.
  <https://en.wikipedia.org/wiki/Ectotherm>

"General Box Turtle Care." Edward M. Craft.
  <http://www.angelfire.com/al/repticare3/page5.html>

"Glossary of Chelonian Terminology." Tortoise Trust.
  <http://www.tortoisetrust.org/articles/glossary.html>

"Guide to Choosing Your First Land-Based Turtle." ATP.
  <http://www.austinsturtlepage.com/Articles/firstlandturtle
  .htm>

"Health Care for Box Turtles." Tess Cook.
  <http://boxturtlesite.info/heal.html>

"Hibernation." Joe Heinen DC.
  <http://aboxturtle.com/hibernation.html>

"Hibernation." Tess Cook.
  <http://boxturtlesite.info/hib.html>

"How Much Do Turtles Cost?" Geoff Williams.
  <http://www.petmd.com/reptile/care/evr_rp_how-much-
  do-turtles-cost#>

"How to Breed Box Turtles." Backwater Reptiles.
  <http://backwaterreptilesblog.com/how-to-breed-box-
  turtles/>

"How to Handle Turtles and Tortoises." R.D. & Patti
  Bartlett.

<http://www.petplace.com/article/reptiles/general/enjoying-your-reptile/how-to-handle-turtles-and-tortoises>

"Importance of Minerals and Vitamins in the Diet." Box Turtle. <http://boxturtlesite.info/min.html>

"Indoor Enclosures for Box Turtles and Other Moisture Loving Chelonians." Box Turtle. <http://boxturtlesite.info/indoor.html>

"Is a Box Turtle a Good Pet for My Child?" Box Turtle World. <http://www.boxturtleworld.com/box-turtle-care/box-turtles-as-pets-for-kids/>

"Keeping Turtles as Pets." Dog Breed Info Center. <http://www.dogbreedinfo.com/pets/turtle.htm>

"List of Turtle Diseases Illnesses and Injuries." Caring Pets. <https://www.caringpets.org/how-to-take-care-of-a-turtle/health/diseases-illness/#deformed-shell>

"Mesic Habitat." Wikipedia. <https://en.wikipedia.org/wiki/Mesic_habitat>

"New Study Recommends Taxonomic Revision of the Genus Terrapene." Box Turtles. <http://www.boxturtles.com/new-study-recommends-taxonomic-revision-of-the-genus-terrapene/>

"Ornate Box Turtle Breeding and Hiberation." Ian Jessup. <http://www.reptilesmagazine.com/Ornate-Box-Turtle-Breeding-And-Hibernation/>

"Reasons pet turtles and tortoises are awesome." Whitney Cox. <http://www.sheknows.com/pets-and-animals/articles/1036209/reasons-pet-turtles-and-tortoises-are-awesome>

"Selecting a Healthy Box Turtle." Box Turtle Care and Conservation. <http://boxturtlesite.info/sel.html>

"Signs of Illness." Jo Heinen DC. <http://aboxturtle.com/boxturtlehealthissues.htm>

"The Law and the Tortoise." Tortoise Group. <http://tortoisegroup.org/care/the-law-the-tortoise/>

"Thinking about a pet turtle?" Turtle Rescue League. <http://www.turtlerescueleague.com/pet-turtles/thinking-about-pet-turtle>

"Turtle." Wikipedia. <https://en.wikipedia.org/wiki/Turtle>

"Turtle & Tortoise Terms." All Turtles. <http://allturtles.com/turtle-terms/>

"Turtle Adoption." Turtle Rescue League. <http://www.turtlerescueleague.com/pet-turtles/turtle-adoption>

"Turtles as Pets." Indiana Department of Natural Resources. <http://www.in.gov/dnr/fishwild/3327.htm>

"Turtles as Pets: Is a Turtle the Best Pet for Me?" Pet Education.

<http://www.peteducation.com/article.cfm?c=17+1797&aid
=946>

"Turtles – Box- Feeding." VCA Animal Hospitals.
<http://www.vcahospitals.com/main/pet-health-
information/article/animal-health/turtles-box-
feeding/1052>

"Turtle Cost." Cost Helper Pets & Pet Care.
<http://pets.costhelper.com/pet-turtle.html>

"Turtle Shell Peeling." Turtleholic.
<http://www.turtleholic.com/turtle-shell-peeling/>

"What do Box Turtles Eat?" Box Turtles.
<http://www.boxturtles.com/what-do-box-turtles-eat/>

"What Does It Mean When A Turtle Sheds?" Pets on
Mom.Me. <http://animals.mom.me/mean-turtle-sheds-
3001.html>

"Wildlife as Pets." Massachusetts Energy and Environmental
Affairs. <http://www.mass.gov/eea/agencies/dfg/dfw/fish-
wildlife-plants/wildlife-as-pets.html>

More Titles Available...

Feeding Baby
Cynthia Cherry
978-1941070000

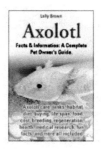

Axolotl
Lolly Brown
978-0989658430

Dysautonomia, POTS
Syndrome
Frederick Earlstein
978-0989658485

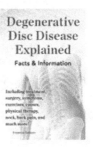

Degenerative Disc
Disease Explained
Frederick Earlstein
978-0989658485

Sinusitis, Hay Fever,
Allergic Rhinitis Explained
Frederick Earlstein
978-1941070024

Wicca
Riley Star
978-1941070130

Zombie Apocalypse
Rex Cutty
978-1941070154

Capybara
Lolly Brown
978-1941070062

Eels As Pets
Lolly Brown
978-1941070167

Scabies and Lice Explained
Frederick Earlstein
978-1941070017

Saltwater Fish As Pets
Lolly Brown
978-0989658461

Torticollis Explained
Frederick Earlstein
978-1941070055

Kennel Cough
Lolly Brown
978-0989658409

Physiotherapist, Physical
Therapist
Christopher Wright
978-0989658492

Rats, Mice, and Dormice
As Pets
Lolly Brown
978-1941070079

Wallaby and Wallaroo Care
Lolly Brown
978-1941070031